HOMING
Jen Southern & Samuel Thulin

Preston, 2016

Homing

Jen Southern & Samuel Thulin

Published by In Certain Places, in 2016.

Edition of 150 copies.
ISBN 978-0-9930498-2-8

Designed by: Serena Pollastri
Photographs of objects: Jonathan Kemp
Photographs of Homing and France: Jen Southern, Samuel Thulin and Charles Quick.

Published to coincide with the exhibition *Homing*, May – November 2016, commissioned by: In Certain Places and Preston Remembers supported by the Heritage Lottery Fund.

Further information and audio-visual documentation of the work:
www.incertainplaces.org/homing

Technology platforms developed by: Media Innovation Studio
http://mediainnovationstudio.org/

With thanks to: Lancashire Infantry Museum and Harris Museum & Art Gallery and all those who read letters for *Homing* from: The North West Officers' Training Regiment; 4th Battalion, The Duke of Lancaster's Regiment; Students of the Acting course, University of Central Lancashire; Students of the Academy of Live and Recorded Arts, North West.

Project supported by:

Foreword
Elaine Speight

Homing is a sonic artwork which extends between different people, places and times. Experienced through headphones and responsive to movement, it generates an intimate, immersive and emotional landscape, in which us, them, here, there, past and present collide. It is also, simultaneously, a site-specific work. Alongside wider and very current connotations about the significance of 'home' within areas of conflict, the title also refers to the location of the work within the north England city of Preston - a city from which the owners of 1,956 names chiselled into the walls of the Harris Museum departed for the hardship and horrors of World War One battle grounds across the English Channel. The situated nature of the work is significant because it makes the abstract specific, and reminds us, in the words of geographer Ed Casey, of 'the stabilizing persistence of place as a container of experience'[1]. For young men in the trenches, Preston represented a site of continuity and safety amongst the unpredictability of war. Yet, their actions, while altering the city in profound and painful ways, also secured its future as the place we know today.

This understanding of place as the product of human activities, memories and relationships has been central to Jen Southern and Samuel Thulin's approach to *Homing*, which has been developed in collaboration with groups, individuals and institutions from across Preston and beyond. Commissioned by In Certain Places in partnership with Preston City Council and the Preston Remembers project, and supported by the Heritage Lottery Fund, *Homing*

---

[1]   *Edward. S. Casey, 1987, Remembering: A Phenomenological Study. Bloomington: Indiana University Press. p186*

4 also builds upon a series of other artworks, events and urban design projects which, over the last five years, have explored and enhanced the social and architectural significance of Preston's Cenotaph. Designed by Sir Giles Gilbert Scott, the monument was unveiled in 1926 as a physical reminder of the sacrifices made by Preston soldiers. Yet, as an empty tomb it is essentially a site of absence. In *Homing*, the Cenotaph becomes a type of anti-transmitter, blocking out communication with the violent hiss of white noise and exposing the disruptions and disconnections which punctuate a place. In doing so, it emphasises the fragility of safety and belonging, and the ongoing need for openness, hospitality, tolerance and exchange within and between our places, if we are all to feel at home.

Elaine Speight is a research fellow at University of Central Lancashire, where she curates In Certain Places.

The Maintenance of Fragments

Jen Southern & Samuel Thulin

When we arrived at the Thiepval memorial in France it was covered in scaffolding for centenary renovations, and the wind blowing through it created a haunting drone. On the day we first tested the sound recordings for *Homing* the flag market was disrupted for re-surfacing works. Later, visitors reported the ways that a funfair, Preston Pride and Armed Forces Day overlapped with their listening experiences. These interruptions remind us that unexpected sensory experiences are often produced by the ongoing happening of the local. Through *Homing* we aimed to use the immediacy of sensory descriptions and sound to connect past experiences of war to the here and now.

Fragmentation and partial records of events often figured in our early research. Neither the archives at the Lancashire Infantry Museum and Harris Museum & Art Gallery, where the objects in this book are from, nor the sounds that comprise the *Homing* exhibition are complete or fully intact. A series of personal letters ends abruptly with a newspaper obituary. Pieces of dried heather drop out of a folder. You hear the beginning of a letter but not the end. They are partial narratives that *Homing* makes manifest, playing on their combination of intensity and fragility. The archival objects act as remnants of social relations that were stretched and transformed by historical and geographical demands. Similarly the audio for *Homing* arises from relations generated by temporal and spatial mobility. Field recordings and sonified GPS data of our trip to the Somme battlefields bring out the distant present while the reading of archival letters by young people living in Preston and the surrounding area today embody and give voice to the nearby past.

6 The images in this book are a visual equivalent of the locative audio work, a series of fragments taken from the archives and assembled with images from France and Preston, each chosen for its connection to a different sensory perspective. They are both military and homely, and range from delicate bows and glitter on greetings cards to photographs of aerial targets, from hand drawn images of buildings to wrecked Zeppelins and ships. Materials such as silk, stone, paper, metal and heather sit together in sunlight and dark cloud. The figures of flight, travel and distance permeate the selections.

The technology behind *Homing* was made in collaboration with the Media Innovation Studio at UCLan who developed a bespoke mobile phone app using 'Estimote' Bluetooth beacons as a way of triggering audio experiences in both indoor and outdoor spaces. The operation of the beacons in situ was not-completely tameable as their response to weather, other networks, and the devices carried by passers-by added an extra layer of interference to *Homing*, extending the tension between clear communication and its inevitable fragmentation over time and space. Moving around Preston's Flag Market and the Harris Museum, the listener to *Homing* does not find neat-and-tidy documents of the past or distant, but instead activates a field of multiple layers of fragmentation and interference still at play.

Jen Southern is an artist and lecturer in Fine Art and New Media at Lancaster University. She is the Director of the mobilities lab at the Centre for Mobilities Research.

Samuel Thulin is an artist and postdoctoral fellow at the Centre for Mobilities Research at Lancaster University.

Close to Home

Dominic Smith

The word punctum in its most literal sense means 'a point'. It can be used when describing a sharp point or when describing a precise absence, such as a blind spot in our vision (Lacrimal punctum), or the removal of specific text from a document (Punctum delens). *Homing* explores these missing spaces, adding to our understanding of the lives of soldiers during World War One. By taking part in *Homing* via headphones and a locative audio device you build a unique narrative that connects the memorial sites to a contemporary personal experience. The work takes place in the combined memorial space of The Roll of Honour in the Harris Museum & Art Gallery, the Flag Market and the Cenotaph in Preston city centre.

Homing began via an exploration of the archives at the Lancashire Infantry Museum with artists Jen Southern and Sam Thulin trying to understand how soldiers connect with home, tracing methods back from current day to the First World War. They came across letters, sent with care to and from the trenches from people maintaining deeply personal connections during a period of great individual and national change.

Following the end of World War One there were many disagreements on the form that memorials should take. There was no historical precedent in existence. In May 1919 the Carlisle Journal noted that a 'fundamental difficulty' of war memorial schemes was finding 'a suitable means of expression' which would reconcile all views, and many places were 'finding great difficulty in discovering a satisfactory solution to the problem.'[2] This problem was

---

2   *Carlisle Journal, 27 May 1919*

resolved to a certain extent via representations of scale, as we see in large lists of names, and architecturally via space in the case of Sir Edward Lutyens' Cenotaph design. Lutyens made use of a design element called 'entasis'. This means that the vertical sides of the Cenotaph are not parallel. If they continued indefinitely they would converge, connecting at a point three hundred metres above ground.

The use of entasis became a common theme in First World War memorials, and Preston's Cenotaph (designed by Sir Giles Gilbert Scott) also makes use of Lutyens' entasis design strategy. It creates a projected, imagined space as an expression of collective loss, it presents a space that can be understood by the eye. *Homing* expands this tradition by creating a relationship with space that can be understood by the ear. It connects all parts of the memorial space, adding personal and emotional weight via the intimacy of spoken words.

You connect with the work from the point at which you collect the *Homing* device and walk towards the Role of Honour in the stairwell of the Harris Museum. The layered, heavily textured sounds present you with a suggested landscape. Standing in front of the names of soldiers that didn't return from the war you hear sounds transition to distant machinery, rain, footsteps, crows and passing horses. A connection is made with the names on the wall and a moment in time. The narrative begins and you notice the effect your position is having upon the arrangement of sounds and voices you can hear. The changing soundscape encourages you to meander through the museum and outside towards the Flag Market. You become aware that your movements are impacting upon the narrative. Just as you are being drawn into a line of dialogue, a few steps forward can bring interference, overlapping tones and a new narrative. It is as if the conditions are just right to pick up distant voices on a shortwave radio. This creates a sensitivity to your surroundings and movement through space. You slow down, stand still and listen carefully.

In making the work the artists began connecting the location of the letter writers and the distance that the correspondence travelled by visiting World War One memorials and cemeteries in France, collecting precise location data and field recordings. The title of the work originates from communication and locative technologies used at the time. This would have included the use of *homing* pigeons and aerial targeting technologies. But there is also a sense in this work that the humanity and personal integrity present in the letters has found its way home via the artwork. The letters have in some ways mirrored the meandering journey a messenger pigeon would take when finding its way home. Soldiers were not allowed to keep correspondence, yet many letters were found after the war and were donated to archives. They have finally found us, having been brought back to life via *Homing*.

As you continue your exploration you move towards the Cenotaph and the work changes. You hear a tonal, sonic representation of the location data that combines your point in space with data collected at Thiepval memorial in France. It silences the narrative with shifting static and interference. The presence of the Cenotaph silences the voices and leaves the listener with a unique moment of contemplation. This is the critical twist in *Homing*, a technology designed to tell us where we are in the world is being used to create an opportunity for a deeper personal understanding of where others have been and what it meant to them. You stand there and consider the reasons for the existence of the memorial. It is a precise moment, a punctum in which all lines connect in a projected space.

As we return to the museum the void is filled by voices once again and we have a sharper awareness of the sensory aspects of the letters. People are writing home about experiencing the cold, the mud, the sounds and smells. We are connected by the everyday experience and language shared by people in the midst of extraordinary circumstances. The prevailing message is one of uncertainty, love and hope.

Dominic Smith is an artist and curator developing a number art and technology based projects in the UK and Europe.

With regards to Homing, from the Edwardian Postcard Project

Julia Gillen

Experiencing *Homing* from the perspective of researching Edwardian postcards coloured the lenses and filters through which I thought, saw, heard and felt *Homing*.

Homing is an imaginative multisensory project. It is more freeing than many encounters with artistic works in that you yourself feel that you have agency in interacting with the work in different ways. As you move, the whole experience changes, sometimes flickering, sometimes firmly differently tuned.

Edwardian postcards are visual and verbal texts that seem to speak to us from people over a hundred years ago. Part of the power of *Homing* lies in hearing audible voices. Young people, often with Lancastrian accents, speak out found letters from soldiers in the trenches in World War One. The soundscapes created by Jen Southern and Sam Thulin offer us other experiences evoking connections to the past: wind, rain, whistling, stonework. We think about the past, monuments to the past, and our own thoughts about the Great War. If you've lived in England almost all your life, as I have, then the Great War has always had a presence, just beyond the remembered past of anyone alive in the family, and yet in our backgrounds. It is brought into prominence every November in particular, yet often at other times, such as when I walk into a new village and see its war memorial for the first time.

Edwardian postcards have their own ways of coming alive. Here is one from our collection, dated 8th August 1909, addressed to a Mr A Develin, 69 Hudson St, Preston. We have transcribed its message as follows:

Dear Arthur I hope you enjoyed yourself at the Hop on Monday. I am enjoying myself down here. I have been up the River Dee to Eaton Hall this afternoon. See the Dukes dogs. wish you could see them Hy Cheetham.

Eccleston Ferry on the Dee, Chester.

Harry Cheetham sounds almost breathless at the end in his excitement at the Duke's dogs. Thinking about them as he writes brings Arthur almost into his presence, an effect noted in many kinds of correspondence including postcards, letters and today's communications by Esther Milne[3]. This postcard became more vivid when I found Arthur Develin at this address in

3 Esther Milne, 2010, Letters, Postcards, Emails: technologies of presence. New York: Routledge

the 1911 census. He was living with his father-in-law, Ebeneezer Haworth, his 14 year-old son, Thorp, already working as an errand boy, and his wife Florence.

The 1891 census revealed that Arthur was no stranger to a multi-generational household. His widowed mother, Hope, had another son and daughter living with her, plus a daughter in law and two grandchildren. The family had strong overseas connections: Hope herself had been born in Malta, as had her oldest son, John. John was a sergeant with the Royal Engineers; his children had been born in India.

It might have seemed inevitable then that Arthur Develin enlisted in the Royal Engineers during the Great War. He was wounded and came home to Preston to die at the age of 31 years and 30 days at Avenham Lane, as recorded in a partially burnt British Army Service Record. We do not yet know what happened to him in the Great War, in what condition he came home and quite why he died. He had served in the 571st (Devon) Army Troops company and 4/2nd Lowland Field Company. In the archives I found also a form completed by him at the time he enlisted. He recorded Preston as his home and that he had married Florence there in 1904.

Five years after that then, while Harry Cheetham was away, they had gone to a "hop", a colloquial name for a dance. The music that accompanied their dancing might perhaps infuse the *Homing* soundscape, in the middle of the night, when nobody is listening. I am perhaps lucky to be researching the postcards of the Edwardian period before the outbreak of war. But the knowledge of what happened next deserves to be remembered. *Homing* offers an experience that we can hear, see and think about in our own ways.

Julia Gillen
Director, Edwardian Postcard Project, Lancaster University.

List of images

1. Greetings card, Harris Museum & Art Gallery, Preston.

2. Newspaper clipping, Captain B. Harris, Lancashire Infantry Museum.

3. Trenches at Newfoundland Memorial Park, Beaumont Hamel, France.

4. Greetings Card from Captain Rudolph Ord, Lancashire Infantry Museum.

5. Homing, Preston, 2016.

6. Photographs sent to Captain R. Ord, Lancashire Infantry Museum.

7. Homing, Preston, 2016.

8. Thiepval Memorial, France.

9. Letter with bullet hole, to Private J.W. Hargreaves, Lancaster Infantry Museum.

10. Drawing by Lieutenant Colonel Brereton

Fairclough, Lancashire Infantry Museum.

11. Detail of 'Target - Aulnoye Railway Junction'. Harris Museum & Art Gallery.

12. Drawing by Lieutenant Colonel Brereton Fairclough, Lancashire Infantry Museum.

13. Detail of 'Target - Le Quesnoy Railway Station' Harris Museum & Art Gallery.

14. Drawing by Lieutenant Colonel Brereton Fairclough, Lancashire Infantry Museum.

15. Detail of 'Target- Petit Maubeuge Railway Station' Harris Museum & Art Gallery.

16. Watercolour by Lieutenant Colonel Brereton Fairclough, Lancashire Infantry Museum.

17. Zepp Wreckage postcard, Harris Museum & Art Gallery.

18. Scaffolding at Thiepval Memorial, France.

19. Zepp Wreckage postcard, Harris Museum & Art Gallery.

20. Homing, Preston, 2016.

21. Zepp Wreckage postcard, Harris Museum & Art Gallery.

22. Homing, Preston, 2016.

23. Silk memorial bookmark, Harris Museum & Art Gallery.

24. Torn postcard, Harris Museum & Art Gallery.

25. Fragment from HMS Lion that took part in the Battle of Jutland. Harris Museum & Art Gallery.

26. Handwritten message, Captain L. Crawford, Lancashire Infantry Museum.

27. Main engine ball-bearing from a Zeppelin. Harris Museum & Art Gallery.

28. Landscape diagram, Captain L. Crawford, Lancashire Infantry Museum.

29. Heather sent to Captain R. Ord, Lancashire Infantry Museum.

30. Caterpillar Valley Cemetery, France.

31. Hand drawn map, Captain L. Crawford, Lancashire Infantry Museum.

32. Railway Hollow Cemetery, France.

33. Envelope from convalescent hospital, Captain R. Ord, Lancashire Infantry Museum.

34. Peronne Road Cemetery, France.

35. Luggage Label, Captain R. Ord, Lancashire Infantry Museum.

36. Greeting card, Harris Museum & Art Gallery.

Cover images: Homing, Preston, 2016.

A VALENTINE WISH FROM PRESTON

Nightingale memories

From Mr M. V. B. Hill

Sir, The recent correspondence on this subject reminds me of the nightingales 60 years ago singing before the attack on the Messines Ridge. This was on June 7. They were about one mile behind the front line and there seemed to be a nightingale in every bush singing at the top of his lungs, until the largest mine of the war went off and the battle began, at 3.10 am.

Yours faithfully,

M. V. B. HILL,

16 Great College Street,

Westminster, SW1.

"The Times"

June 4ᵗʰ 1977.

1917

GREETINGS

RNS P.
FEATHER E. A.   HUDSON W. E.   PEARSON G.   SPENCE F.   WEEDER W. J.   WILLIAM
RTON C. F.   FEATHER E.   HUGHES W.   PEPLOW C.   SPENCER E.   WHARTON G. H.   YOUNGER R.
RTON W.   FEATHER R.   HUNT G. L.   PERKIN C.   SPITTLEHOUSE I.   WHARTON F.

FEATHER   HURST A. B.   PETTY H.   STAINSBY I.   WHATMOUGH W.   LCE SERJEANT

TTERFIELD   FENNELL J. W.   INGHAM A.   PHILLIPS C.   STAMBEY W.   WHEAT E.
J. R.   FERGUSON J.   INGHAM A.   PHILLIPS O.   STANSFIELD W.   WHEELHOUSE G.   BONE H. G.
KIN J.   FERNSIDES F. D.   ISHERWOOD E.   PICKARD A.   STANSTELD W.   WHIPP H.   EDWARDS R.
ALDRED I. J.   FIELDEN W. 4862   ISHERWOOD A. E.   PICKERING M. H.   STAVELEY S.   WHITAKER E.   NOTMAN W.
ALLAGHAN A.   FIELDEN W.   JACKSON C. H.   PICKLES H.   STEAD H.   PENNY C.
ALLENDER   202148   PICKUP J.   STEED E.   WHITBREAD A.   PUGH C. W.   PEARSON H.
ALBERT E.   FINAN J.   JACKSON R.   PILLING C.   STEER S.   WHITE R.   SEMPLE D.   RAMSAY F.
ARLTON F. G.   FIRTH G.   JAGGER J. H.   PINDER H. J.   STEPHENSON H. R.   WHITEHEAD G.   TELFORD J.   SCRIVENS J. S.
ARROW   FIRTH J.   JENNINGS A. G.   PLATT W.   STIRK W.   WHITELEY A.   SEWELL J.
ARROLL   FLETCHER S. T.   JENNINGS C.   PLUMBLEY J. A.   STITSON A.   WHITELEY H.   CORPORAL   SHERWIN T.
ARTLIDGE J. A.   FOLEY M.   JENNINGS M.   POOLE J.   STOCKS F.   4691   ALLEN J. T.   SHORTER T.
ARVLEY R.   FOSTER F.   JESSON F. W.   POWIS J. T.   STOKES W. J.   WHITELEY J. E.   ARMSTRONG T. G.   SIMPSON R. I.
ASEY F.   FOSTER L.   JOHNSEY W.   PRESTON J. E.   STONE W. J.   12795   ASPINALL G.   SMITH E.
ASTLE J.   FOWLER A. P. P.   JOHNSON A.   PRIESTLEY E. J.   STOTT G.   WHITELEY J.   BALDERSTONE E. A.   SOWERBY F. E.
HALLENGER   FOX J.   JOHNSON J. G.   PRIESTLEY F.   STREET G. F.   WHITELL J.   BELL S. J.   SPARK F.
J. L.   FRANCIS H.   JONES E.   PRIESTLEY J.   SUNDERLAND G.   WHITEOAK T. C.   BOWNES T. A.   STAINTON J.
HAMBERLAIN S.   FREEMAN C. H.   JOWETT A.   QUARTON C.   SURTEES H.   WHITTAKER J. A.   BRIANTON G.   STEELE W.
HAMBLER   FRENCH J.   JULIAN A.   RAISTRICK E.   SUTCLIFFE F.   WHITTERON R.   BROCKBANK W.   STEWARTSON T.
HAPMAN   FRYER G. M.   KAY B.   RALPH C.   SUTCLIFFE H.   WIDDOWSON E.   BRYAN C.   STOCK R.
HATWIN   FURNISS A.   KAY J. E.   RATTIGAN P.   SUTCLIFFE J.   WIDDUP A.   BURGESS W. J.   SUNDERLAND K.
HESTER T. W.   GARSIDE H.   KAYE D.   RAWLING G.   SUTCLIFFE V.   WIDDUP J.   CHARLTON T. W.   TAYLOR P.
HIPPENDALE   GASCOIGNE G.   KAYE E. 5763   RAYNER W.   SWIFT S.   WIGGLESWORTH H.   COLCLOUGH C.   TRAVIS C. E.
GEBB J.   KAYE E. 23988   READYHOUGH T.   SYKES A.   WILD J.   FISHER J. B.   VICKERS P.
LAPHAM A. G.   GIGGLE A.   KAYE O.   REDDISH H.   SYKES H.   WILKINSON B.   GRAHAM W.   WEBB E.
LAPHAM J. R.   GILDERDALE D.   KEEGAN J.   REDFERN H.   SYKES H. 3971   WILKINSON J. W.   HOGBEN E.   WHITMORE J.
LAREY F.   GILL W.   KELLETT C.   RENARDSON F.   SYKES H. 241581   WILLIAMS A.   HOPE J. E.   WILLIAMS D. B. M.
LARK A.   GLEDHILL H.   KELLY G. H.   RENNISON G.   TAYLOR F.   WILLIAMS E.   HUTCHINSON H.   WILSON A.
ARK D. B.   GLEDHILL W. A.   KELLY T. F.   RHODES A.   TAYLOR H. 17917   WILLIAMS J. T.   JACKSON G. A. J.   WILSON F.
J. W. H. B.   GLEDHILL W. B.   KENNEDY T.   RHODES C.   TAYLOR H. 18368   WILMAN C.   JACKSON G. R.   WRIGHT L.
GLEN A.   KERSHAW F.   RICHARDSON A. C.   TAYLOR J. I.   WILSON H.   LEIGHTON R.
GLEW S.   KIDDY A.   RICHARDSON H.   TEAL G.   WINDSOR A. E.   LEMON W. H.   PRIVATE
GLOVER J.   KILMISTER W. T.   RIDLEY S.   TEAL W. H.   WINTERBOTTOM J.   McINTOSH E. C. M. M.   AINSCOUGH J.
GOLDSBROUGH F.   KINDER S.   RIGBY C. T. W.   TEALE A.   WISHART D. M.   MEYERS T.   AINSWORTH A.
GOLDTHORPE A.   KNAGGS C. G.   RILEY A.   TEMPERTON B. S.   WOMERSLEY B.   PARK S.   AINSWORTH A.
MERSALL A. E.   LACEY G. W.   ROBERTS J.   TEMPEST A.   PASSCO S. F. G.   ALLEN F.
DALL E.   LAHIVE J.   ROBINSON A.   TEWKESBURY F. R.   WOOD C.   RITCHIE R.   ALLEN G. V.
LAWTON F. W.   ROBINSON C.   THEODORE T. F.   WOOD E.   ROBERTS W. P.   ALLEN P. H.
COLE D. J.   LAWTON W.   ROBINSON F.   THOMAS J.   WOOD F. D.   SAUNDERS T. W.   ALLPORT F.
CODRING   LAYCOCK W.   ROBINSON H. M. M.   THOMPSON A.   WOOD H. J.   SLATER R.   ANDERSON A.
WEDE H.   LAZENBY J.   ROBINSON H. S.   THOMPSON C. F.   WOOD H. M.   STEWARD W. J.   ANDREWARTHA
LEE S.   ROBINSON J. W.   THOMPSON E.   WOOLLEY B.   TEMPERLEY T.   ANDREWS H. I.
GGETT A.   ROBINSON J. W.   10896   WORTH R.   TOWNLEY W.   APPLETON T.
ROBINSON S.   THOMPSON E.   WRIGGLESWORTH   D. C. M.   ARGENT G.
J. W.   ROBINSON W.   15780   S.   TRIMBLE J. G.   ARMSTRONG S.
RODGERS G.   THOMPSON H.   WAYMAN W.   ARMSTRONG
LUBS   ROGERS W.   THOMPSON W. H.   WRIGHT F.   WILKINSON J.   ASBRIDGE W.
OCKSHOTT   ROOKE H.   THORNE H. S.   WRIGHT J.   WILSON N.   ASCROFT H.
OLLIER G.   GREEN   ROSE W. T.   THORNTON J. R.   WRIGHT W.   WREN R. J.   ASHMORE H.
LINGWOOD N.   GREENWOOD   ROSS H.   THORPE H.   WYATT E. J.   ASKEW H.
OLLIS D. K.   BOTTOM   THORPE N. W.   WYNN M.   LCE CORPORAL   ASPEY H.
OMASKEY   GREENWOOD   BURKE J.   YATES H.
SERVED A.   LONSDALE   THORPE T. E.   YATES J. W.   AIREY W.   ASPEY L. F. E.
KERSHAW   GRIMES   ATKINSON J.   ATKINSON
ONWELL J.   GRUNDY R.   LORD   BORDER   REGIMENT   ATKINSON J.   ATKINSON
OOPER A.   HAIGH F.   LORD   LORIMER   BAGLEY J.   ATKINSON
OOPER J.   HAIGH G.   CAPTAIN   LIEUTENANT   BALL E.

92 Lawdor St
Farnworth
Nr Bolton

Dear Brother

Just a few
lines hoping [to find]
you in the [best of]
health as it leaves me
at present. Mother and
Edith went down to
tea to my Grandma's
on Sunday. Dear [brother]
I wish you [were]
home for the wakes
I used to pull my
face when you had
me stood on the
market holding

LOCRE

MUD

NP.
28/2/15

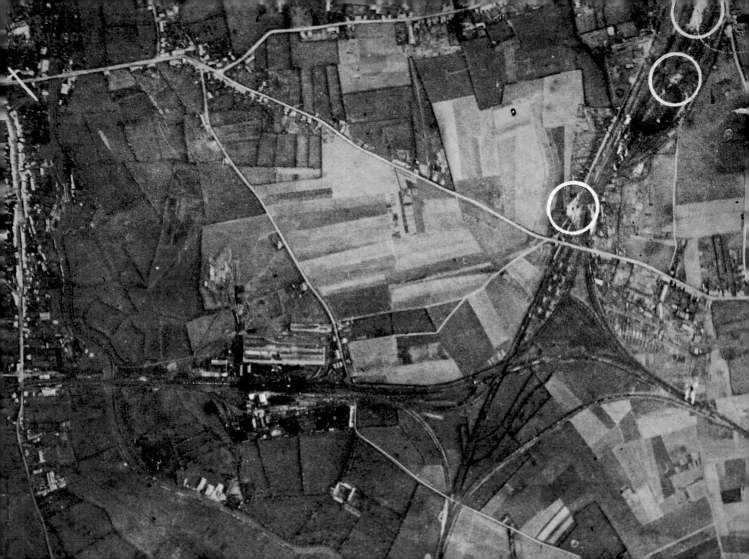

AN ARTILLERY BILLET. *Vlamertinghe.*

A. CHATEAU

3?
BOSCHE
WILFUL DAMAGE
BARASTRE
28
9
17

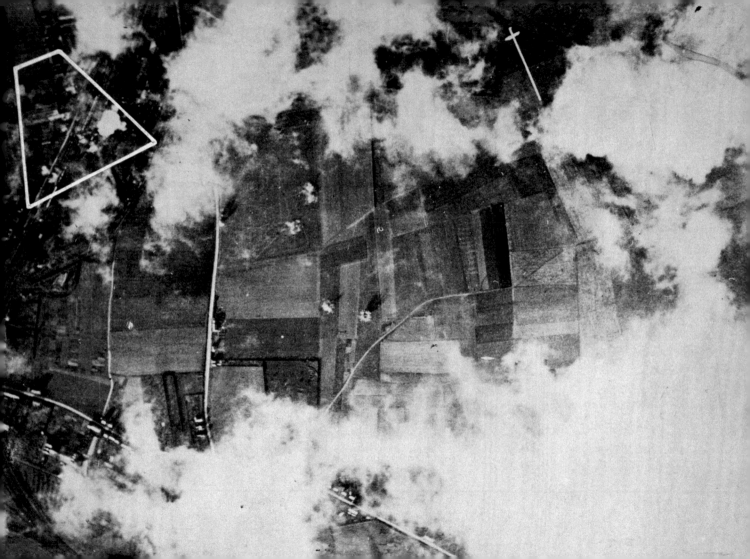

Nth Wales
A Billet
26
9
77

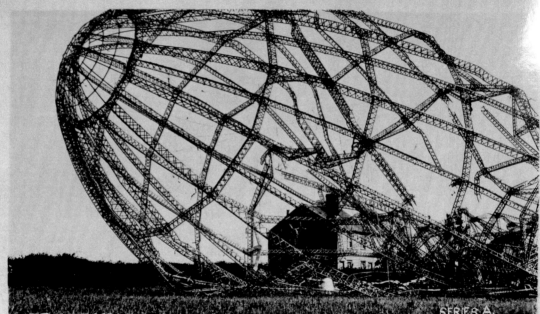

ZEPP WRECKAGE

ZEPP WRECKAGE.

SERIES. A

CROWN COPYRIGHT RES.

ZEPP WRECKAGE

SERIES IX.

CROWN COPYRIGHT RES.

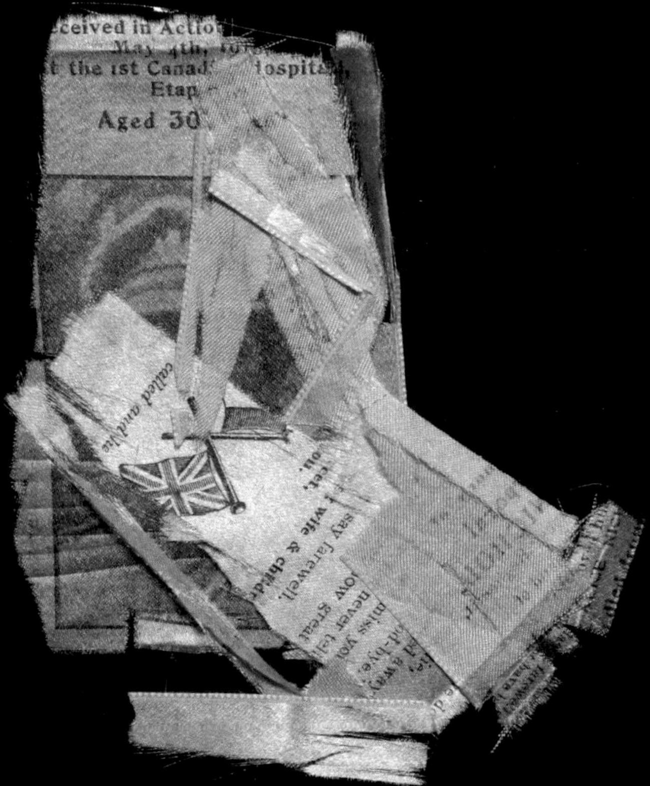

ceived in Action
May 4th,
t the 1st Canad... Hospital,
Etap

Aged 30

called antiihe

your

wife & child

ay farewell,

never great

miss you

good-bye

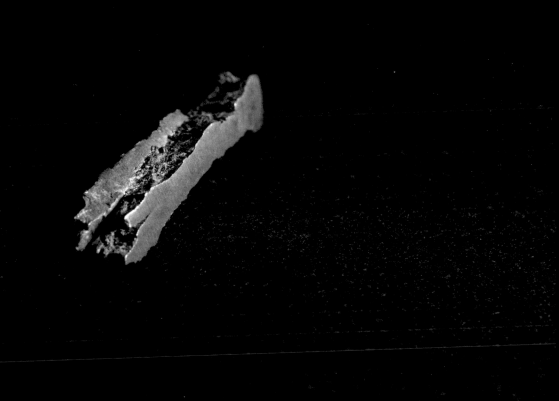

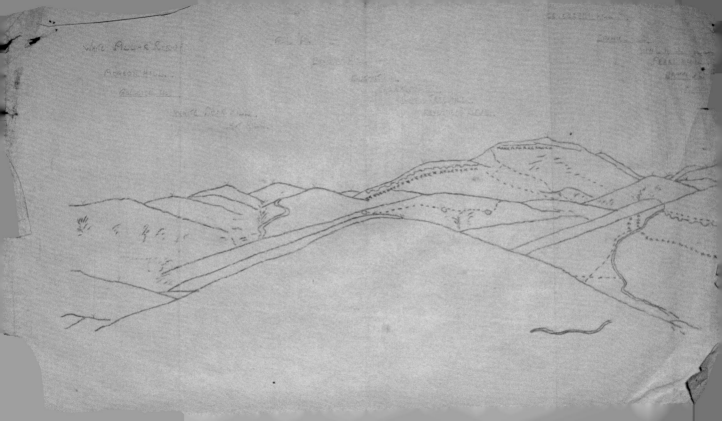

BRISTOL
11. 30 PM
27 SEP 16

Captain N. Ord
1/4 Royal N. Lancash Regt.
B. E. F.
France.

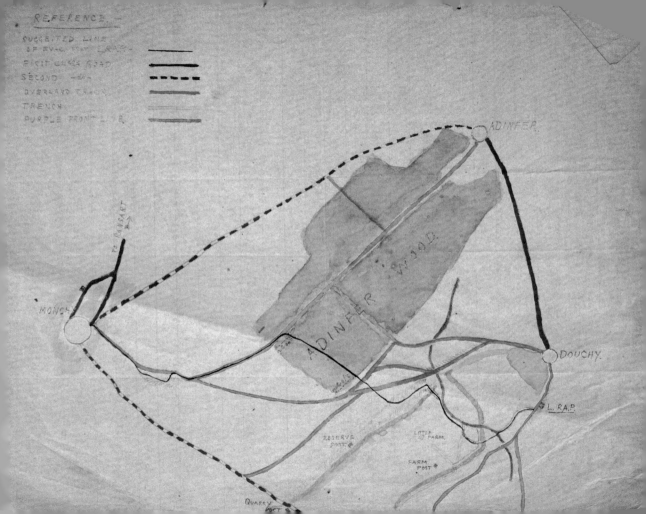

REFERENCE —

SUGGESTED LINE
OF EVACUATION &c.

FIRST CLASS ROAD

SECOND —do—

OVERLAND TRACK

TRENCH

PURPLE FRONT LINE.

ADINFER

To BAILART

MONCHY

ADINFER WOOD

DOUCHY

L. R.A.P.

RESERVE
POST

LITTLE
FARM.

FARM
POST

QUARRY
POST

A Kiss from France